The Name for Your Baby

The Name for Your Baby

By *Jane Wells and Cheryl Adkins*

Westover
Publishing Company

A Media General Publication
Richmond, Virginia

ISBN   0-87858-020-4

Jacket design by L. A. Strickland
Illustrations by T. F. Hale

To Stephen
May he be a gardener
of Joy and a harvester
of Love

1

HE CAN'T REMAIN
"WHAT'S-HIS-NAME"
FOREVER

So you're going to have a baby! Congratulations! What a wonderfully exciting experience is soon to be yours. A baby brings such joy into life that your days will be filled with the sheer wonder of him or her. Even more mystifying is that *you* will miraculously become a parent. What a strangely challenging word "parent" is! You'll soon be dumbfounded by the responsibilities, and you'll soon experience the first great privilege of being a parent—naming your baby.

Naming your baby is a responsibility as well as a privilege (there are always catches to everything). After all, your baby will be stuck with his name for a whole lifetime, and its choice should be no spur-of-the-moment whim on your part. Although your baby will be tiny and helpless, think of him as an individual, as a *real* person. It's more difficult than it sounds.

Try to imagine your baby as a businessman thirty years from now. Will his name be a help or a hindrance? If that's too difficult, try to imagine him seven years from now when he

---

goes to school. Will he be chided or embarrassed by his name? Will he be able to spell it? Will the teacher be able to pronounce it?

Still can't imagine your baby so far in the future? Then try to imagine Uncle Mike and Aunt Sadie coming to see you at the hospital. They congratulate you and stare lovingly at the baby. But they ask you to repeat baby's name six times, and they *don't* have a hearing problem. Your problem may be just beginning.

How can you avoid the problems in naming your baby? Not so simple. Choosing a name is a difficult duty. Like everything else, there are many ways to choose a name for your baby. Some ways are quite good; others are perfectly terrible. Try our "common sense" rules and use your own intuition.

And, by the way, once you have chosen the name, don't let anyone talk you out of it. Don't listen to Uncle Oscar or Aunt Sarah. Follow your own good sense.

Now just sit back and wait patiently for . . .

J. W.
C. A.

The How, What, Where, Why, and Who of Naming Your Baby

"Tell your name the livelong day"
—*Emily Dickinson*

4

Everyone will have an opinion about how you should choose
a name for your baby. We have listed a few commonsense
rules that might be considered.

How does it sound?

In naming a baby, one of the first things new parents usually
do is to listen to how the name sounds with their own
surname. This is a good idea. There are some basic rules
that might help you find a name that fits your last name
like a glove.

The length of your surname should determine the length of
Baby's name. A long first name can really almost lengthen a
short last name right before your eyes.

Lee Jones
Timothy Jones

The latter is much more interesting in terms of both sound
and sight. The real key to the sound of names is the number
of syllables in your last name. You can make a most attractive
name if you vary the number of syllables in the first, middle
and last names. For example, if your last name is "Pitt," the
name "Jane Lynn" can only stress the single syllable in your
last name. Wouldn't "Jennifer Pitt" be more attractive? If
"Jane Pitt" was your great grandmother's name and you
want to use it, try a middle name with three syllables or more.

Jane Jennifer Pitt
1   3   1
Jane Lavinia Pitt
1   4   1

5

If you have a two-syllable last name and like a two-syllable first name, use the middle name to make it sound more interesting. Use either a longer or shorter middle name.

Cheryl Lynn Walcroft
2   1   2
Cheryl Elizabeth Walcroft
2   4   2

Just as changing the number of syllables can make a name sound more interesting, alliteration can also make a name more easily pronounced and remembered. For example, the name "Jennifer Jones" matches good syllable planning with the same beginning letter and sound. This name is blended beautifully. It is very difficult to use alliteration well, and, as in all good things, a little goes a long way. We had a student in our class named Roberta ReBow. With a name like that we were certain she was destined to be a stripper. To avoid such problems, say the name to yourself, or have someone say it to you. Decide if the names sound well together or whether you have gone too far.

While we are on the subject of initial sounds, what about those of you who are expecting twins? Who ever said that twins had to have rhyming names or names that begin with the same letter? Nobody, that's who. Your twins are two definite individuals who, through no decision of their own, are born at relatively the same time. All their lives they will have to share their birthdays, their toys, their parents, and even their faces. Why make life *more* of a dual existence by giving them matching names? Remember, each twin is a really unique individual. You would never expect them both to follow the same profession. Okay, so make them individuals from the start by spending time to give them each unique names.

What does it mean?

Juliet might not have seen the importance of a name when it came to Romeo, but as a parent you are realizing it. Perhaps the meaning of a name is of little importance; but, somehow it is always interesting to discover what your own name means. Although we would never suggest that you base the selection of your baby's name on that point alone, you might want to use the meaning of the name to break a tie between two favorites.

Where did it originate?

It is impossible to trace a name back to the time it was first used. Since it is difficult to give each name a place of origin, we have settled for the first time we can find the name recorded. Most boys' names can be traced to their ancient roots in Greek, Roman, or Hebrew civilizations. Modern languages change names. The changes in spelling have occurred because of the now-common use of nicknames and language differences. For example, "John" can be said "Jon," "Jose," "Ivan," "Jean," "Ian," "Johan," "Hans," or "Giovanni" to name only a few. Many other boys' names are taken from common last names.

Girls' names are almost always feminine variations of masculine names. For example, "Catherine," "Charleen," and "Charlotte" are all variations of "Charles." The only really feminine names are those associated with flowers (Rose), jewels (Ruby), and virtues (Faith).

Why spell it that way?

There is a strong case for choosing the most common spelling
of a name. Much confusion is caused when a name is spelled
in any manner other than the most common. Anyway, why
make things more difficult for your child? "Janeen" is just as
nice as "Gynene" and an awful lot easier to spell, too.

Did you know that there are eighteen spellings for the name
Katherine? We have listed the two most common. In the name
lists, the most common spelling is listed first with the more
unusual following afterward.

If you have a long or difficult last name, a strangely spelled or
unusual first name will only complicate the name further.
Simplicity is a good rule of thumb. You will really help your
child by keeping his name as simple, in terms of spelling, as
possible.

Just imagine what would happen if your Gynene or Katharyne
was enrolled in a large first grade class. The teacher would
probably ask each child his name and write it for him on the
name tag. More than once, a child has proudly displayed his
first attempt at writing his name, only to have Mother shriek
because the spelling is wrong. How would you like to have to
spell *your* name every time you say it? It's not much fun.

When you consider the spelling of your baby's name, you
need also to consider the initials. Some people think that it is
good luck if the baby's initials spell a word. Maybe that's true,
but make sure you know what that word is before anyone else
spots them. It wouldn't be very pleasant to be surprised by
the fact that Baby's initials form a word of questionable taste.
Initials can spell a word; just make sure it's a word that won't
prove embarrassing.

Who did you name him or her for?

Family names are great, but don't be trapped into them. If you don't like the name "Egbert," don't let your baby be hooked with it either. Forget that Uncle Egbert mentioned you in his will. Your baby's name is your decision; nobody should make the decision for you.

Family pressure can be pretty stiff when it comes to a baby's name. This may be your first big chance to exert the new independence that parenthood brings. Let your baby's name reflect what you want, as parents. Uncle Egbert won't mind, and a grateful son or daughter will thank you for it later on.

Many families like to pass a Christian name from one generation to the next. Daddy may be "Edward James Martin, III." It would be nice to have an "Edward James Martin, IV." You must think about the pros and cons to this before making a snap decision. First of all, do you like the name? If you don't, stop right there. If it seems to please you, consider the nickname that your husband uses. If he is called "Ed," and Grampa is called "Eddie," what will you call the new baby? It is important that the baby have a name, if only a nickname, of his own. You might consider using the middle name or going to a lesser used nickname for Edward, like "Ward" or "Teddy."

It has recently become fashionable to use family names or maiden names as babies' middle names. This seems like an extremely good idea, for it assures the family of its importance while delegating that importance to a second place. Also, many children appreciate the fact that they are named for someone special or that they carry a favorite family name. If such names are used, again be sure to consider the sounds and syllables. A difficult middle name goes well with a more simple first and last name.

Susan Scheaffer Wells
Catherine Clay Westover

While on the subject of middle names, a few suggestions can be offered. First of all, spend just as much time lovingly selecting the middle name as you do with the first. We look at our roll books and wonder at the numbers of "Anns," "Maries," and "Lynns." They, along with "Lee" and "Kay" are common middle names and just about as interesting as reading the dictionary. Your child's middle name should require as much thought and love as his first name. Use a family name, a maiden name, or a name you just happen to like — but let those names reflect your baby's new personality.

Nicknames seem to occur whether they are planned or not. Take a look at our list of names to find the nicknames commonly associated with proper names. Think about which nickname *you* would prefer. If you make the decision about your child's nickname ahead of time, nobody will make the choice *for* you later on. Heaven only knows how many Megs became Peggys because Grandma — God love her — saw baby first. If you consider a nickname ahead of time, you can make your feelings known, and nobody will accidently rename your child. If you absolutely don't like nicknames, let that feeling be known, too.

It is also important to listen to how a nickname sounds with your last name. Your child will use his nickname for much of his life. Margaret Pargee is a fine name. But Margie Pargee sounds terrible, and Peggy Pargee isn't much better. This Margaret should definitely be a Meg.

In choosing your baby's name, family name or not, it is good to see if it has any unpleasant connotations of which you are unaware. Fidel is a perfectly good name, but it could let your child in for a lot of teasing when he's older. Samantha is a beautiful name that has been worn rather thin by the onslaught of a particular television series. Of course, by the time your baby goes to school, the witch named "Samantha" may be forgotten, and Fidel may have realigned Cuba with the United States.

Names can also have pleasant connotations and associations. One of the most popular names in the 1930s was "Melanie." The popularity of the name was directly timed to the release of *Gone With the Wind* in which Melanie was a sweet, loving character. The girls in *Little Women* were long immortalized to the point that any girl bearing the name "Jo" was considered a tomboy. Extremely popular names can cause some problems for a child if there are other children with the same name in class with him for a few years. So, somewhat unthinkingly, his teacher may give him a different nickname just to keep the children straight.

The currently popular names in our classrooms are:

Boys		Girls	
David	5	**Laurie or Lori**	4
Michael	4	**Theresa or Teresa**	3
Chuck	2	**Donna**	2

You might like to consider now if the name truly reflects the baby's sex. If Marion is a family name and you can't use it as the middle name, give your son a good solid masculine middle name—like "Sam." Then he can make the choice later on.

Now that you have thought about the length, sound, meaning, derivation and connotation of the name you like, you are ready to give it the final test.

1. **Write it down.**
2. **Say it out loud.**
3. **Have someone read it to you.**

Naming your baby is a responsibility that every parent should cherish. We hope that you will explore the name lists, use our rules, and use your own common sense in choosing a name for your new baby. Good luck!

THE BABY'S NAME

The boy's name I chose: **The girl's name I chose:**

Date: Date:

Why I chose this name: **Why I chose this name:**

Baby arrived on:
Time: Weight:
Place:

Baby's name will be:

Baby's nickname will be:

Baby was Christened on:
                    place:
          Godparents:

The baby's sign of the Zodiac is:

Father's sign: **Mother's sign:**

SIGNS OF THE ZODIAC

CAPRICORN
The Goat
Dec. 22–Jan. 21

Color:	Blue
Ruling planet:	Saturn
Personality traits:	Selfish, cautious, conservative, persistent, quiet
Congenial signs:	Taurus and Virgo

AQUARIUS
The Water Carrier
Jan. 22–Feb. 21

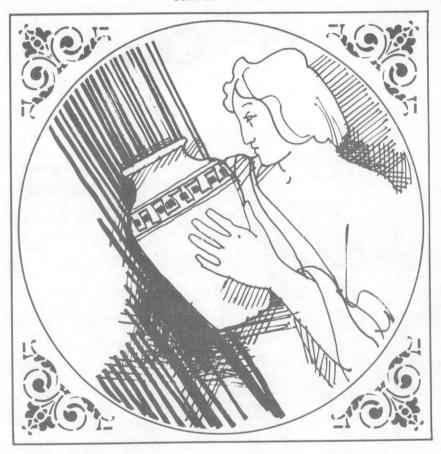

Color:	Blue
Ruling planet:	Uranus
Personality traits:	Faithful, honest, kind, forgetful, intuitive
Congenial signs:	Libra and Gemini

PISCES
The Fishes
Feb. 22–Mar. 21

Color:	Purple
Ruling planet:	Neptune
Personality traits:	Reverent, kind, idealistic, affectionate, forgiving
Congenial signs:	Capricorn and Taurus

ARIES
The Ram
Mar. 22–Apr. 21

Color:	Red
Ruling planet:	Mars
Personality traits:	Enterprising, stubborn, disorganized, aggressive
Congenial signs:	Sagittarius

TAURUS
The Bull
Apr. 22–May 21

Color:	Yellow
Ruling planet:	Venus
Personality traits:	Conservative, practical, trustworthy, jealous, generous
Congenial signs:	Capricorn and Virgo

GEMINI
The Twins
May 22–June 21

Color:	Violet
Ruling planet:	Mercury
Personality traits:	Witty, intelligent, flighty, fickle, adventurous, emotional
Congenial signs:	Aquarius and Libra

CANCER
The Crab
June 22–July 21

Color:	Green
Ruling planet:	Moon
Personality traits:	Sentimental, sensitive, uncertain, moody, domestic
Congenial signs:	Pisces and Scorpio

LEO
The Lion
July 22–Aug. 21

Color:	Orange
Ruling planet:	Sun
Personality traits:	Arrogant, impatient, organized, healthy, trusting
Congenial signs:	Sagittarius and Aries

VIRGO
The Virgin
Aug. 22–Sept. 21

Color:	Violet
Ruling planet:	Mercury
Personality traits:	Critical, sympathetic, intelligent, petty, dutiful
Congenial signs:	Taurus and Capricorn

LIBRA
The Scales
Sept. 22–Oct. 21

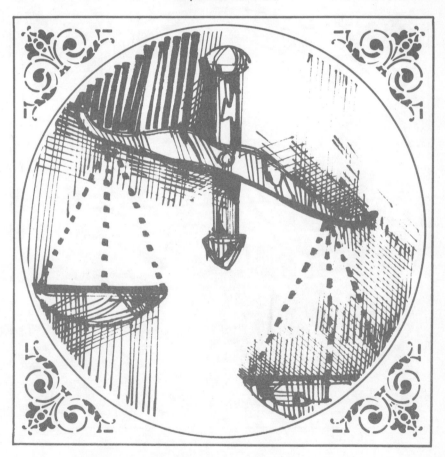

Color:	Yellow
Ruling planet:	Venus
Personality traits:	Charming, honest, sincere, artistic, vain
Congenial signs:	Aquarius and Gemini

SCORPIO
The Scorpion
Oct. 22–Nov. 21

Color:	Red
Ruling planet:	Mars
Personality traits:	Honest, extreme, witty, alert, sarcastic, secretive, procrastinating
Congenial signs:	Cancer and Pisces

SAGITTARIUS
The Archer
Nov. 22–Dec. 21

Color:	Light purple
Ruling planet:	Jupiter
Personality traits:	Generous, curious, impulsive, philosophical, tactless
Congenial signs:	Aries and Leo

MONTH	BIRTHSTONE
January	Garnet
February	Amethyst
March	Aquamarine
April	White sapphire
May	Emerald
June	Alexandrite
July	Ruby
August	Peridot
September	Blue sapphire
October	Opal
November	Golden sapphire
December	Blue zircon, diamond

	BIRTH FLOWER
January	Carnation
February	Violet
March	Jonquil
April	Daisy
May	Lily of the Valley
June	Rose
July	Larkspur
August	Gladiolus
September	Aster
October	Calendula
November	Chrysanthemum
December	Holly

Names for Your Baby Girl

"This is my name forever, and my memorial unto all generations."
Exodus 3:15

A

ABAGAIL	(Abby, Gail) "My father is joy"; Hebrew
ADA	(Aida, Eng.) "Prosperous, happy"; Old English
ADELAIDE	(Addie, Adela, Adel) Noble; Old German
ADELBERTA	(Bertie) Bright; Old German
ADELE, ADELIA	(Del) Noble; Teutonic
ADELEPHA	Sisterly; Greek
ADELINE	Lengthened form of Adele; Became famous in 1903 song
ADELLE	(Adele) French equivalent of Ethel, Noble; French
ADOLPHA	Wolf; Germanic
ADONICA	Sweet; Latin
ADORA	Gift; Greek
ADRIENNE	French, derived from Latin
AGATHA	(Aggie) Good, kind; Greek
AGNES	(Aggie) Chaste; Greek
AILEEN	Light bearer; Anglo-Irish (Form of Helen)
AIMEE	Beloved; Latin
ALAYNE, ALAINE	(Allie) Light; Latin
ALBERTA	(Albertina, Albertine) Noble, brilliant; Teutonic
ALBINA	White; Latin

ALDA	Wise, rich; Old German
ALDITH, ALDYTH	Old; Germanic
ALDORA	Gift; Latin
ALETHEA	Truth; Greek
ALEXANDRA	(Lexi, Ann, Alexis) "Helper and defender of mankind"; Greek
ALEXIA, ALEXIS	Variations of Alexandra
ALFREDA	Elf; Germanic (Feminine form of Alfred)
ALICE, ALICIA	(Allie, Elsie) Truth; Greek
ALISON, ALYSON	"Little truthful one"; Irish Gaelic (Form of Alice and Louise)
ALMA	Cherishes and nourishes; Latin
ALMEA	(Mea) Highest one; Greek
ALMIRA	Exalted, Arabic; Spanish (Feminine form of Elmira)
ALOHA	Greetings, farewell; Hawaiian
ALTHEA	(Thea) A healer; Greek
ALVA	White; Latin
ALVINA, ALVINIA	Friend; Teutonic
ALYNE	Feminine form of Alan, Latin
AMANDA	(Amy, Mandy) Worthy of love; Latin
AMARYLLIS	A refreshing stream; Greek
AMBER	Amber jewel; Old French

AMEBEL	(Amy) Lovable; Latin
AMELIA	Industrious; Teutonic (Derivation of Emily)
AMETHYST	Gem; Greek
AMY	(Aimee, French) Beloved; Latin
ANASTASIA	(Ann, Stacy) Of the resurrection; Latin
ANDREA	Womanly; Latin
ANGELA	(Angelina, Angelica, Angelique) Lovely angel; Greek
ANITA	Graceful; Spanish (Form of Ann)
ANN, ANNE, ANNA	(Annie, Nan, Nancy, Nanne) Grace; Hebrew
ANNABEL	Beauty; Hebrew
ANNETTE	Grace; Hebrew
ANTOINETTE	French form of Annette
ANTONIA	Priceless; Latin
APRIL	Opening; Latin
ARABELLA	(Bel, Bella) Heroine; Latin
ARIADNE, ARIANE	Holy; Latin
ARLINE, ARLEEN, ARLENE	A pledge; Irish Gaelic
ATHENA	Wisdom; Greek
AUDREY	Noble strength; Old English
AUGUSTA, AUGUSTINE	(Gussie) Exalted; Latin
AVIS	Bird, flight; Latin

B

BABETTE	(Bab) A stranger; Greek
BARBARA	(Barb, Barbie, Babs) Foreign or strange; Greek
BATHSHEBA	Daughter of oath; Hebrew
BEATA	Blessed; Latin
BEATRICE	(Bee, Trixy) "She that makes happy"; Latin
BEDELIA	(Delia) Strong; Old French
BELINDA	(Linda) Pretty; Spanish
BELLE	Beautiful; French
BENEDICTA	Blessed one; Latin
BENITA	The blessed; Latin
BERNADETTE	Brave as bear; French
BERNADINE	Hard; Germanic
BERNICE	Bold; Greek
BERTHA	(Bertie, Berty) Bright; Teutonic
BERYL	Sea-green jewel; Greek
BETH	From Elizabeth
BETTINA	Oath of God; Hebrew
BEULAH	Married; Hebrew
BEVERLY	Dweller at beaver meadow; Old English
BEVIN	Sweet voice; Irish Gaelic
BLANCH, BLANCHE	White; Teutonic
BLOSSOM	A flower; Anglo-Saxon
BLYTHE	Cheerful; Old English

BONITA	Pretty; Spanish
BONNIE	Good one; Middle English
BRENDA	Little raven; Irish Gaelic
BRIDGET	(Biddy) Lofty, august; Irish
BRUNHILDA	Warrior; Old German
BUENA	Good; Spanish
BURNETTA	Little dark one; Old French

C

CAMILLA, CAMILLE	Girl of freedom; Latin, French
CANDACE, CANDICE	(Candy, Candie) Glittering; Greek
CARA	Beloved one; Italian
CARESSE	Endearing one; French
CARISSA	Dear one; Latin
CARLOTTA	Italian (Feminine form of Charles)
CARMEL	Garden; Hebrew
CARMEN	Song; Latin
CAROL, CAREL, CAROLE	(Carrie) Strong and womanly; Latin
CAROLINE, CAROLINA	Strong; Italian-Spanish (Feminine form of Charles)
CAROLYN	Form of Carol
CATHERINE, CATHLEEN	(Cathy, Catty) Pure one; Greek

CATHRYN	(Cathy, Catty) Greek
CECILIA, CECILY	Latin (Feminine form of Cecil)
CELESTE	Heavenly; French
CELIA	Heavenly; Latin
CELISTINE	Heavenly; Latin
CHARISSA	Grace; Greek
CHARLOTTE	Strong; French (Feminine form of Charles)
CHERYL	(Cherry, Cher) May be variant of Caryl or derivative of Cherie
CHLOE	Young, herb; Greek
CHRISTABEL	Christ + Belle
CHRISTINA, CHRISTINE	(Chris, Chrissy, Christie, Tina) Daughter of Christ; Greek
CLARA	Bright, illustrious; Latin
CLARIBEL	Brightly fair; Latin
CLARICE, CLARISSA	Bright; Latin (From Clara)
CLAUDIA	The lame one; Latin (Feminine form of Claude)
CLAUDINE	French
CLEMENTINE, CLEMENTINA	Latin
CLEOPATRA	(Cleo) "Of a famed father"; Latin
COLLEEN	A girl; Irish
CONSTANCE	(Connie) Firmness, constancy; Latin

CORA	Maiden; Greek
CORDELIA	Jewel of the sea; Latin–Welsh
CORINNA, CORINNE	Maiden; Greek
CORNELIA	Latin (Feminine Form of Cornelius)
CRYSTAL	(Chris) Clear; Latin
CYNTHIA	(Cindy) The moon; Greek

D

DAGMAR	Glory of the day; Danish
DAISY	Flower name; Anglo-Saxon
DANA	Feminine form of Dan; Hebrew
DAPHNE	Laurel; Greek
DARLEEN, DARLENE	Darling; Anglo-Saxon
DAWN	To become day; Anglo-Saxon
DEANNA	(see Diana)
DEBORAH, DEBRA	(Debbie) A bee; Hebrew
DEE	(see Diana)
DEIRDRE	Complete wanderer; Irish Gaelic
DELIA	Visible; Greek
DELLA	English, Derivation of Adele
DENISE	Wine and song; French
DIANA, DIANE	Goddess; Latin
DINA	Small; Latin

DINAH	Judged; Hebrew
DOLORES	Sorrows; Spanish
DONNA	Lady; Spanish
DORA	Golden; Latin
DORIS	From the ocean; Greek
DOROTHEA, DOROTHY	(Dot, Dottie, Dolly) "Gift of God"; Greek
DRUSILLA	(Dru) Latin
DULCE	(Dulcie) Charming, dear; Latin

E

EARLENE	Noble woman; Old English
EARTHA	The earth; Old English
EDITH, EDYTHE	(Edie) Rich gift; Anglo-Saxon
EDNA	Young again; Hebrew
EDWINA	Guardian of land; Anglo-Saxon (Feminine of Edwin)
EILEEN	Light; Irish for Helen
ELAINE	(see Helen) French
ELEANOR, ELINOR	(Ella, Ellie, Nell, Nellie) Light; French
ELFRIDA	Good counselor; Old English
ELISE	Consecrated to God; French
ELIZABETH, ELISABETH, LIZABETH	(Bess, Bessie, Betsy, Betty, Elsie, Libby, Lisa, Lizzy, Beth, Liz) Consecrated to God; Hebrew

ELLEN	(see Helen)
ELOISE	(see Louise) French
ELSA	Noble one; Greek
ELVIRA	Well-born; Latin
EMELINE, **EMMELINE,** **EMMALINE** **EMILY**	Industrious one; French
EMMA	(Emm, Emmie) Universal one; Greek
ENID	Woodlark, purity; Celtic
ERLA	Noble; Old English
ERMA, IRMA	Army maid; Teutonic
ERMEN- **GARDE**	Teutonic
ERNESTINE	Earnest one; Greek
ESTELLE	Star; Latin
ESTHER	A star; Hebrew
ETHEL	Noble; Anglo-Saxon
ETTA	(see Henrietta) Little one; Old German
EUDORA	Generous; Greek
EUGENIA	Well-born; Greek
EULALIA	Greek
EUNICE	Happy victory; Latin
EUPHEMIA	Of good report; Greek
EVA	Eve; Latin
EVADNE	Fortunate; Greek

EVANGELINE	Bring good news; Greek
EVE	Life; Hebrew
EVELINA	Life; Latin
EVELYN	Youth; Latin

F

FAITH	(Fay) Faithful; Latin
FANCHON	Free; Teutonic
FAUSTINA	Lucky; Latin
FAWN	Young deer; Latin
FAY, FAYE	Elf; French
FEDORA	Gift of God; Greek
FELICIA, FELICE	Happy; Latin
FELIPA, FILIPA, FILYPA	Horse lover; Latin
FERDINANDA	Adventurer; Teutonic
FERN	From the plant; Anglo-Saxon
FIDELIA	Faithful; Latin
FIFINI, FIFI	(see Josephine) He shall add; Hebrew
FILMA	Misty; Germanic
FIONA	White; Irish
FLAVIA	Blond; Latin
FLORA, FLEUR	Flowers; Latin

FLORENCE, FLORANCE	(Flo, Flossie) Prosperous; Latin
FLORIS	A flower; Latin
FLOYCE	Flourishing; Latin
FORTUNA, FORTUNE	Lucky; Latin
FRANCES	(Franny, Fran) Free; Italian
FRANCINE	Free; Teutonic
FREDERICA	(Fritzi) Peace; Teutonic
FRIEDA, FREDA	Peace; German

G

GABRIELLE	Of God; French
GAIL, GAYLE	My father is joy; Hebrew
GARDENIA	Flower; Germanic
GARLAND	A wreath of flowers; Latin
GAY, GAYE	Merry; French
GENEVIEVE	(Jen, Gen, Gend) Fair girl; Celtic
GEORGETTE	Farmer; Greek
GEORGIA, GEORGIANA	Farmer; Greek
GERALDINE	(Jerry) To rule; Teutonic
GERMAINE	A German; Latin
GERTRUDE	(Gertie, Trudy) Warrior maiden; Teutonic
GILDA	Servant of God; Celtic

GLADYS	(Glad) Lame; Latin
GLENNA	From the valley; Gaelic
GLORIA	Glory; Latin
GODIVA	God, gift; Anglo-Saxon
GOLDIE, GOLDY	Golden-haired; Germanic
GRACE	Favor; Latin
GRACIA, GRATIA	Thanks to the Gods; Latin
GRETA	A pearl; Greek
GRETCHEN, GRETEL	Little pearl; German
GRISELDA	Gray; Teutonic
GUINEVERE	A fair lady; Celtic
GUNHILD, GUNHILDA	Battle; Germanic
GWENDOLYN	(Gwen) Celtic
GWENYTH	Fair; Celtic
GYDA, GYTHA	Gift; Teutonic

H

HAGAR	Forsaken; Hebrew
HALLIE	Feminine form of Hal
HANNAH	Grace; Hebrew for Ann
HARMONY	Harmony; Latin
HARRIET	(Hatty) Feminine form of Harry

HAZEL	A plant name; Anglo-Saxon
HEATHER	Flower; Old English
HEBE	Youth; Greek
HEDDA	Strife; Germanic
HEDVA	Joy; Hebrew
HEDWIG	Strife; German
HEDY	Strife; Germanic
HEIDI	From Adelaide; German
HELEN, HELENA	(Nell) The bright one; Greek
HELENE	Light; Greek
HELGA	Holy; Germanic
HELOISE	Wide; French
HELSA	(see Elizabeth) Hebrew
HENRIETTA	(Etta) Feminine form of Henry
HEPHZIBAH	My delight in her; Hebrew
HERMIONE	Of the earth; Greek
HERTA, HERTHA	Earth; Germanic
HESTHER, HESPER	(Hetty) A star; Persian
HILDA	Battle maiden; Anglo-Saxon
HILDEGARDE	Battle maiden; Teutonic
HILLARY	Joyful; Latin
HINDA	A female deer; Anglo-Saxon
HOLLY	Named for plant; Anglo-Saxon

HONOR, HONORA, HONORE	(Nora, Norah) Honorable; Latin
HOPE	Hope; Teutonic
HORATIA	(see Horace, male)
HORTENSE, HORTENSIA	"A lady gardener"; Latin
HULDAH	A weasel; Hebrew
HYACINTH	(Cinthy) Flower; Greek

I

IANTHE	Purple flower; Greek
IDA	Youthful; Teutonic
IDALIA	A happy one; Latin
IDELLA, IDELLE	A happy one; Latin
ILEANA, ILENE	(see Eileen)
ILKA	A worker; Germanic
ILSA	German for Elsie
IMOGENE	An image; Latin
INA	Praise; Germanic
INEZ	Spanish form of Agnes
INGRID	Beautiful; German
IONE	Island; Greek
IRENE	(Rene, Renie) Peace; Greek

IRIS	Rainbow; Greek
IRMA	Noble; Latin
ISA	Iron; Germanic
ISABEL, ISABELLA	(Belle, Bella) French form of Elizabeth
ISADORA	Gift of Isis; Greek
ISOLDE	Fair; French
IVY	For the plant; Anglo-Saxon

J

JACALYN	May God protect; Hebrew
JACINTA	May God protect; Hebrew
JACQUELINE, JAQUELINE	French, Feminine of Jacob, Jacques
JAMIE	(see James, male)
JAMESINA	(see James, male) Hebrew
JANE	Gift of God; French from Joan
JANET	Gift of God; Hebrew
JANICE	Gift of God; Hebrew
JASMINE	Persian flower name
JEAN, JEANNE	French from John
JEANNETTE	Derivative of Jeanne
JEMIMA	Dove; Hebrew
JENNIFER	(Jenny) Fair lady; Old English
JESSICA	Gift of God; Hebrew

JESSIE	(see Janet) Scottish
JEWEL	A gem; Latin
JILL	Youthful; Old English
JOAN, JO ANNA, JOHANNA	Hebrew, Feminine form of John
JOBINA, JOBYNA	(see Job, male) Hebrew
JOCELIN, JOCELYN	(see Joyce) Latin
JOEL	Goat; Hebrew
JOLETTA	The violet; Latin
JONEA	Gift of God; Hebrew
JOSEPHINE	(Jo, Josie) Feminine form of Joseph
JOYCE, JOY	Joyous; Latin
JUANITA	(Nita) Gift of God; Hebrew
JUDITH	(Judy, Judie, Judi) Praised; Hebrew
JULIA, JULIE	Latin, Feminine form of Julius
JULIANA	Latin, Feminine form of Julian
JULIET	French, diminutive of Julia
JUNE	Feminine form of Junius
JUSTINA	Latin, Feminine from Justin

K

KANA	Wished for; Sanskrit
KAREN	(see Catherine) Danish

KARLA	Man; Germanic
KASIA, KASSIA	Polish form of Katharine
KATHERINE	(Kathy, Kate, Kitty, Katie) Pure; Greek
KATHRYN	(Kathy, Kate, Katie, Kitty) Pure; Greek
KATHLEEN	(from Katherine) Irish
KATRINE	Pure; Greek
KAY, KAYE	(see Katherine)
KELLY	Anglo-Saxon surname
KELLYN	Dream come true; American
KEZIA	Cassia; Hebrew
KIMBERLY	(Kim) (see Kim, male)
KIRETA	Active; Greek
KIRSTEN, KIRSTIN, KRISTIN	A follower of Christ; Latin
KOREN	Maiden; Greek
KYLE	(see Kyle, male)
KYRA	(see Cyrus, male)

L

LALA	A tulip; Slavic
LANA	Wool; Latin
LANETTE	A lane; Old English
LARA	Famous; Latin

LARAINE	(see Lorraine)
LARISSA	Cheerful; Latin
LAURA, LAURETTA, LORA	Laurel, victory; Latin
LAVINIA	A woman of Lavinium; Latin
LEAH	(Lee) Weary; Hebrew
LEILA, LEILAH	Dark as night; Arabic
LELIA	Darkness; Latin
LEMUELA	Dedicated to God; Hebrew
LENA, LINA	(see Helena) Light; Greek
LEODA	Of the people; Germanic
LEONA	The lion; Latin, Feminine form of Leon
LEONARDA	Germanic, Feminine form of Leonard
LEONORA	(Lora) Light; Greek
LESLIE, LESLEY	(Les) Dweller; Celtic
LETA	Joy; Latin
LETITIA	(Letty) Happiness; Latin
LIANE, LIANA	A bond; Latin
LILAC	A flower; Persian
LILIAN	(Lilly, Lil) Lily, Latin
LILIS	For the flower lily; Latin
LILY	For the flower lily; Greek
LINA	(Nickname for Caroline) Germanic

LINDA	Beautiful; Latin
LINNEA	Lime tree; Germanic
LINNET	Idol; Welsh
LISA, LISE	(Diminutive of Elizabeth) Hebrew
LISBETH	(see Elizabeth) Hebrew
LIVIA	The olive; Latin
LIZZIE	Hebrew, diminutive of Elizabeth
LOIS	Pleasing; Greek
LOLA, LOLITA	Spanish, diminutive of Dolores
LORA	Victory; Latin
LORENA, LORNA	Victory; Latin
LORETTA	Victory; Latin
LORINDA LAURINDA	(see Laura)
LORRAINE	Victory; Latin
LOTTA, LOTTY	Germanic, diminutive of Charlotte
LOTUS	For the flower lotus; Latin
LOUISE, LOUISA	(Lou) Glory; Germanic
LUCIA	Latin, Feminine form of Lucius
LUCILE, LUCILLE	Light; French
LUCINDA	(Cindy) Light; Latin

LUCRETIA	Bringer of light; Latin
LUCY	Light; Latin
LUELLA, LOUELLA	(Lou) Expiation; Latin
LUGENE	Well-born; Greek
LULU	(Lu) Pearl; Persian
LUNA	Moon; Latin
LUVENA	Beloved; Germanic
LYDIA	(Liddy) A native of Lydia; Greek
LYNN, LYNNE, LYNNA	(see Lynn, male)

M

MABEL, MABLE, MABELLE	(Mab) Loveable; Latin
MADELINE, MADELEINE, MADELAINE, MADALYN, MADELENE	(Maddie) Magnificent; Hebrew
MADELLA	Magnificent; Hebrew
MADELON	French form of Maude
MADGE	A pearl; Greek, diminutive of Margaret
MADIERA	Place name; Italian or Spanish
MADRA	A mother; Latin
MAE, MAY	Hoped-for child; Latin

MAGDA	(see Madeline)
MAGDALENE	"Belonging to Magdala"; Hebrew
MAGGIE	(see Margaret) A pearl; Greek
MAGNOLIA	For the tree; Hebrew
MAHALA	Tenderness; Hebrew
MAIA, MAYA	Growth; Greek
MAIDENA	Maiden; Germanic
MAIRE	Irish for Mary
MAISIE	Pearl; Scottish for Margaret; Greek
MAJESTA	Queen like; Latin
MALCA	Hard worker; Germanic
MALINA	(see Magdalene) Hebrew
MALVA	Soft; Greek
MALVINA	A chief; (see Melvin, male) Celtic
MAMIE	(see Margaret) Mary
MANDY	Diminutive of Amanda; English
MANETTE	Bitter, wished for; Hebrew
MANON	(see Mary) Pet name for Marianne
MANUELA	(see Emanuel, male)
MANYA	(see Mary) Slavic
MARA	Bitter, diminutive of Mariam; Hebrew
MARALINE	Belongs to Mars; Latin
MARCELLA, MARCELLINA, MARCELLINE	From Mars; Latin

MARCHETTE	Diminutive of Marcia
MARCIA	(see Marsha) Latin
MARELDA	Famous; Germanic
MARETTA, MARETTAE	Against; Hebrew
MARGARET	(Marge, Margy, Peggy, Maggie, Meg) A pearl; Greek
MARGERY, MARJORY	(Marge) (see Margaret)
MARGOT	French for Margaret
MARGUERITE	French for Margaret
MARI	Irish for Mary
MARIA, MARYA	(Ria) (see Mary)
MARIAN, MARION	French for Mary
MARIANNE, MARIANNA	(see Mary and Ann) French
MARIBEL	(see Mary and Bel)
MARICE	Bitter; Hebrew
MARIE	(see Mary) French
MARIETTA	(see Mary) Italian
MARIGOLD	For the flower
MARILLA	Diminutive for Mary
MARILYN	(see Mary)
MARINA, MARINITA	Of the sea; Latin

MARIS	(see Marina)
MARJORIE	(see Margery)
MARKA	Feminine form of Mark or Marcus; Bavarian
MARLA	Bavarian diminutive of Mary
MARLENA, MARLEEN	(see Mary)
MARMARA	Bright; Greek
MARNA	(see Marina)
MARTA	German form of Martha
MARTHA	(Marty) Lady, mistress; Aramaic
MARTINA	Feminine form of Martin
MARVA	Feminine form of Marvel
MARY	New Testament form of Miriam; Hebrew
MATHILDA, MATELDA	(Tilly, Matty, Patty) Mighty bottle maid; Teutonic
MAUD, MAUDE	Diminutive of Mathilda
MAURA, MAURYA	(see Mary) Irish
MAUREEN	(see Mary) Irish
MAURITA	Black; Latin
MAVIS	Thrush; French
MAXINE	Great; Latin
MAY, MAE	Diminutive of Mary

MAYDA, MAIDA	A maiden; Old English
MEDA	A ruler; Greek
MEG	(see Margaret)
MEGAN, MEIGHAN	(see Margaret) Irish
MEHITABEL	(Hitty) A favorite of God; Aramaic
MELANIE	Dark; Greek
MELANTHA	Dark; Greek
MELBA	Place name
MELICENT	Teutonic
MELINDA	(Lin) (see Belinda) Old English
MELISSA	(Missy) All; Greek
MELLA	(see Carmela)
MELODY, MELODIE	Song; Latin
MELOSA	Melody; Latin
MELVA	(see Melba)
MELVINA	A handmaiden; Celtic
MERCEDES	Mercies; Spanish
MERCY	(see Charity) Latin
MEREDITH	(Meri) Wonderful; Welsh
MERIS, MARIS	Of the sea; Latin
MERIT, MERRITT	Merit; English

MERLE	A blackbird; Latin
MERRILL	Feminine form of Merrill
MERRY, MERRIE	Merry; Old English
MERYL	(see Muriel)
META	Diminutive of Margaret
MICHELLE, MICHELE	(Shelly, Micky) Feminine form of Michael; French
MIGNON	Dainty, darling; French
MILDRED	(Milly, Millie) Strong and mild; Anglo-Saxon
MILLICENT	(Millie) Work, strength; Teutonic
MILLIE	(see Mildred)
MIMI	Nickname for Margaret, Marie; Hebrew
MINA, MINNA	Nickname for Wilhelmina
MINERVA	(Minnie) Love, remembrance; Latin
MINNETTE, MINNIE	Mind; Greek
MIRANDA	(Randy) Admirable; Latin
MIRIAM	Original name for Mary; Hebrew
MIRTH	Happy; Old English
MITZIE	(see Mary)
MODESTA	Modest; Latin
MOIRA	Irish
MOLLY	Irish for Mary
MONA	Noble; Irish

MONICA	Adviser; Latin
MORNA	Beloved; Irish
MOSELLE	Feminine form of Moses
MUIRE	Irish for Marie
MURIEL, MERIAL, MERIEL	Sea-bright; Greek
MUSA	A muse; Latin
MUSETTE	A little muse; French
MYRA, MIRA	Wonderful; Latin
MYRNA	(see Merna) Celtic
MYRTILLA	(see Myrtle)
MYRTLE	Plant name; Greek

N

NADA	Hope; Slavic
NADIA	Hope; Slavic
NADINE	Hope; Slavic
NAN	(see Ann, Nancy)
NANCY	(Nan, Nance) Form of Ann
NANELLE	(see Nancy) Hebrew
NANNETTE	Grace; French for Ann
NAOMI	My sweetness; Hebrew
NARA	Joy; Celtic
NARCISSA	Beauty; Greek

NARDA	The spikenard; Persian
NATA	A dancer; Sanskrit
NATALIA	(see Natalie) Latin
NATALIE	(see Noel, male) French
NATASHA	(see Natalie) Russian
NATHANIA	Feminine form of Nathan
NEBULA	A cloud; Greek
NEDA, NEDDA	Feminine form of Edward; Old English
NEDRA	From the novel *Nedra*
NEETA	(see Nita)
NELL, NELLY, NELLIE	Diminutive of Ellen and Helen
NELLYN	A friend; Germanic
NEOMA	A new moon; Greek
NERINE	A child of the sea; Greek
NERISSA	A child of the sea; Greek
NESSIE	(see Agnes)
NESTA	Innocent; Latin
NETTA, NETTY, NETTIE	(see Jeanetta)
NEVA, NEVADA	Snow; Latin
NEYSA	(see Agnes) Slavic

NICOLE, NICOLETTE	(Nicky) Victory; Greek
NIKA	Victory; Greek
NILA	The river; Egyptian
NINA, NYNA	Diminutive of Anne; French
NINETTE	Diminutive of Ann
NINON	French for Ann
NITA, NETTA	Abbreviation of Juanita; Spanish
NOEL, NOELLA, NOWELL, NOELLE	Feminine form of Noel; French
NOLA	Diminutive of Olivia
NONA	(Nonie) The ninth; Latin
NONIE	(see Nona)
NORA, NORAH	Irish form of Honora
NORBERTA	(Bertie) From Njord, from Norse, God of the sea; Scandinavian
NOREEN, NORINE	The sea; Irish
NORMA	(see Norman, male) Latin
NOVA	New; Latin
NUNCIATA	Brings news; Latin
NYDIA	A nest; Latin

O

OBELIA	A pillar of strength; Greek
OCTAVIA	The eighth; Latin
ODELIA	Rich; Germanic
ODETTE	French for Ottilie
OLA	Feminine form of Olaf
OLGA	Holy; Russian, Norse
OLIVE	An olive; Latin
OLIVIA	An olive; Latin
OLYMPIA	Heavenly; Greek
ONA	The one; Latin
OPAL	Name of a jewel; Latin
OPHELIA	Help; Greek
ORA	Golden; Latin
ORIANA	Rising; Latin
ORIEL, ORIOLE	Golden; Latin
ORLENA	Golden; Latin
ORPAH	A young stag; Hebrew
OTTILIE	Fatherland; Germanic
OUIDA	(see Louise) French

P

PAGE, PAIGE	From a knight; English
PALLAS	A virgin; Greek
PALMYRA	(Myra) From the tree; Latin

PAMELA	(Pam, Pammy) Sweet; English
PANDORA	(Pandy, Dora) A gifted one; Greek
PANPHILA	Loved; Greek
PANSY	From the flower; French
PARTHENIA	A virgin; Greek
PATIENCE	(Pate, Pat) Long-suffering; Latin
PATRICIA, PATRISHA	(Pat, Patty, Trish, Trisha) Feminine form of Patrick
PATSY, PATTY	Noble; Latin
PAULA	Feminine form of Paul; Latin
PAULINA	Small; Latin
PAULINE	(see Paulina) French
PEACE	Peaceful; Latin
PEARL	A pearl; Latin
PEGGY	(see Margaret) Greek
PEGEEN	Irish diminutive for Peg
PELAGIE	A weaver; Greek
PENELOPE	(Penny) A weaver; Greek
PENNY	(see Penelope)
PEONY	From the flower; Greek
PEPITA	Feminine form of Joseph; Spanish
PERDITA	The lost one; Latin
PERFECTA	Perfect; Latin
PERIAN	(see Perry and Ann) Anglo-Saxon

PERNELLA	(Nell) A young woman; Celtic
PERRY	Nickname for Pearl
PERSIS	A Persian woman; Greek
PETRINA	(Pet, Rina) A rock, feminine for Peter; Greek
PETUNIA	For the flower; American Indian
PHEMIE	From Euphemia
PHEODORA	A gift of God; Greek
PHILA	Love; Greek
PHILANA, PHILLINA, PHILANA	(Phil) Lover of mankind; Greek
PHILBERTA	Brilliant; Germanic
PHILLIPPA	Feminine form of Philip; Latin
PHILOMELA	(Phil) Lover of the moon; Greek
PHILOMENA	(Phil) Lover of mankind; Greek
PHOEBE, PHEBE	Shining; Greek
PHYLLIS	(Phyl) A green bough; Greek
PIA	Pious; Italian
PLACIDA	Calm, quiet; Latin
POLLY	Diminutive of Mary
POMONA	Fruitful; Latin
POPPY	For the flower; Anglo-Saxon
PORTIA	Wife of the noble; Latin

PRIMA	The first; Latin
PRIMROSE	(Rose) For the flower; Latin
PRISCILLA	(Pris, Prissy) Former; Latin
PRUDENCE	(Pru, Prudy) Discretion; Latin
PRUNELLA	(Nellie, Pru) Plum-colored; Latin
PSYCHE	Soulful; Greek

Q

QUARTILLA	From Quartres
QUEENIE, QUEENA	Diminutive of queen; Germanic
QUERIDA	Loved one; Spanish
QUINNE	Feminine form of Quinn; Irish
QUINTA	The fifth one; Latin

R

RACHEL	An ewe; Hebrew
RADELLA	To protect; Germanic
RAE	(see Rachel)
RAISSA, RAYSA	Exalted; Hebrew
RAMONA	Feminine form for Ramon; Spanish
RANA, RAINA	Royal, rose; Sanskrit
RANDA	(Randy, Randie) Feminine form of Randall

RAPHAELA, RAFAELA	Healed by God; Hebrew
RAYA	Feminine form of Ray
REBA	Diminutive of Rebecca
REBECCA	(Becky, Reba) Yoke; Hebrew
REGINA	(Gina) Queen; Latin
REINA, REINE	Poised; Latin
RENA	Song; Hebrew
RENATA	Reborn; Latin
RENE	(see Irene)
RENEE	Reborn; Latin
RENITA	Self-poised; Latin
RHEA	Earth; Greek
RHODA	A rose; Greek
RHONDA	Grand, elegant; Welsh
RICA	Diminutive of Frederica
RICARDA	Hard, Feminine form of Richard; Germanic
RICHENDA, RICHARDA	Hard; Germanic
RIMA	Diminutive of place name Riolama
RINA	Diminutive of Irene
RITA	Pearl; Italian
RIVA	To dream; French
ROANNA, ROANNE	(see Rose and Ann)

ROBERTA	(see Robert)
ROBIN, ROBINA	(see Robin, male)
ROCHELLE	Small rock; French
RODERICA	Feminine form of Roland
ROLANDA	Feminine form of Roland
ROLLA	Feminine form of Rolf
ROMA	For the city Rome; Latin
ROMOLA	A Roman; Italian
RONA	(see Ronald)
RONALDA	(see Ronald)
RONNIE, RONNI	Nickname for Roanna or Veronica
ROSA, ROSE	A rose; Latin
ROSABEL	Fair rose; Latin
ROSALIA, ROSALIE	A rose; Latin
ROSALIND	Pretty rose; Spanish
ROSALINE	Pretty rose; Spanish
ROSAMOND	Horse protection; Teutonic
ROSEANNA	(see Rose and Anna)
ROSEMARY	From the plant
ROSETTE	(see Rose)
ROSINA, ROSITA	(see Rose)

ROWENA	A friend; Celtic
ROXANA, ROXANE	(Roxy) The dawn; Persian
ROXANNA, ROXANNE	Respelling of Roxane
RUBETTA, RUBETTE	Red—for the gem; Latin
RUBY	Red—for the gem; Latin
RUDA, RUDELLE	Famous; Germanic
RUE	Named for the plant, rue; Greek
RUPERTA	For Roberta; Germanic
RUTH	Beauty; Hebrew

S

SABINA	A Sabine woman; Latin
SABRINA	Latin for the River Severn, England; Latin
SACHA	A helper; Greek
SADELLA, SADELLE	A princess; Hebrew
SADIE	A princess, diminutive of Sarah; Hebrew
SALINA, SALENA	Salty; Latin
SALLY	(see Sarah) Peace; Hebrew
SALOME	Peaceful; Hebrew
SAMARA	A guard; Hebrew

SAMELA, SAMELLA	Feminine form of Samuel; Hebrew
SANDRA	(Sandy, Sandie) See Alexandra; Greek
SAPPHIRA	For the gem, sapphire; Greek
SAPPHIRE	For the gem; Greek
SAPPHO	The tenth muse; Greek
SARA, SARAH	(Sadie, Sal, Sally) A princess; Hebrew
SARITA	A little princess; Hebrew
SAVINA	From an ancient Italian tribe; Latin
SEBASTIANA	Feminine form of Sebastian; Greek
SECUNDA	The second one; Latin
SEEMA	A treasure; Hebrew
SELA	A rock; Hebrew
SELDA	(see Zelda)
SELENE, SELENA	The moon; Greek
SELIMA	Peace; Hebrew
SELINA	Moon; Greek
SELMA	Divine, feminine for Anselm; Germanic
SEPTIMA	The seventh; Latin
SERAPHINE	An angel; Hebrew
SERENA	Serene; Latin
SHANNON	From a surname; Irish
SHARI	Form of Sara; Hungarian

SHARON	(Shara, Shari) A great plain; Hebrew
SHAWN	Irish form of John, also used for feminine name
SHEBA	From the Bible
SHEERA	Song; Hebrew
SHEILA	(see Celia) Irish
SHELAH	Requested; Hebrew
SHELBY	Homestead; Old English
SHELLEY	Shell island; English
SHERRY	Cherished one; From the French Cherie
SHERYL, SHARYL	Love; Greek
SHIRLEY	(Shirl) From the district meadow; Old English
SHOSHANNAH	Rose; Hebrew
SHULAMITH	Peace; Hebrew
SIBYL, SYBIL	Prophetess; Greek
SIDNEY, SYDNEY	(Sid) (see Sidney, male) Celtic
SIDONIA, SIDONIE	(Sadie) An enchantress; Latin
SILVIA, SYLVIA	(Silvie) Forest; Latin
SIMONE, SIMOANE	(Simmy, Mona) One of gracious hearing, feminine for Simon; Hebrew
SIVIA	Doe; Hebrew

SONDRA	(see Alexandra)
SONJA, SONIA, SONYA	(Sonny) Wisdom; Greek
SOPHIA	(Sophie) Wisdom; Greek
SOPHRONIA	Sensible; Greek
STACY	(see Anastasia)
STAR, STARR	Star; English
STELLA	A star; Latin
STEPHANA	Feminine form of Stephan; Greek
SUSAN, SUSANNE, SUSANNAH	(Sue, Suzy, Suzi, Su-Ann) A lily; Hebrew
SUZANNE	(Suzi) French for Susan
SYDEL, SYDELLE	From Sadie or Sydney

T

TABITHA	(Tabby) Gazelle or deer; Aramaic
TACITA	The silent; Latin
TALITHA	A damsel; Aramaic
TALLULAH, TALLULA	Running water; American Indian
TAMA, TAMAH	Astonishment; Hebrew
TAMARA, TAMAR	(Tammy) Palm tree; Hebrew

TANYA, TANIA	For Russian Tatiana; Latin
TARA	Crag; Gaelic
TECLA	Divine; Greek
TEMPERANCE	Moderation; Latin
TERESINA	(Terry, Tes) To reap; Italian and Spanish
THADDEA	Praise; Hebrew
THALIA	Blooming; Greek
THEA	Goddess; Greek
THEADRA	Tragic woe; Greek
THECLA, THEKLA	Divine; Greek
THEDA	(see Theodosia)
THELMA	Nursling; Greek
THEMIS	Justice; Greek
THEODORA	Gift of God; Greek
THEODOSIA	Gift of God; Greek
THEOPHILIA	Loved by God; Greek
THERESA, TERESA, THERESE	(Terry, Tess) The harvester; Latin
THIRZA	Pleasant; Hebrew
THOMASA, THOMASINA	Feminine form of Thomas; Latin
THORDA	Feminine form of Thor
TILDA, TILLY	For Matilda, mighty; Germanic

TINA, TEENA	Diminutive for Christina
TOBEY	A dove; Germanic
TONYA, TONIA	(Toni) Feminine form of Tony or Anthony
TRISHA, TRICIA	(see Patricia)
TRIX, TRIXY	(see Beatrice)
TYBALLA	Bold; Teutonic

U

UDA	Wealthy; Germanic
UDELE	Wealthy; Anglo-Saxon
ULA	A jewel from the sea; Celtic
ULRICA	Rich; Teutonic
UNA	One; Latin
UNDINE	Watery; Latin
URANIA	Heavenly; Greek
URSA, URSEL	She-bear; Latin
URSULA	She-bear; Latin

V

VALENCIA, VALENTIA	(Val) Strong; Latin
VALENTINA	(Val, Tina) Healthy; Latin
VALERIE	(Val) Valor; Latin
VALONIA	A dweller in the valley; Latin

VALORA	Brave; Latin
VANESSA	(Van) Butterfly, See Van and Essa; Greek
VANIA	Gift of God, Russian feminine form of John; Hebrew
VARINA	A stranger; Greek
VASHTI	A star; Persian
VEDA	Knowledge; Sanskrit
VELEDA	Wisdom; Germanic
VELIKA	Great; Slavic
VELMA, VELMN	Feminine form of William; Germanic
VENETIA	Selling; Latin
VERNA	Born in the spring; Latin
VERONICA	(Ronnie) A virgin; Latin
VESTA	A virgin; Latin
VICTORIA	(Vicky, Tory) Victory; Latin
VIDA	Feminine form of Davida
VIDONIA	A vine; Latin
VINCENTIA	To conquer; Latin
VINITA, VENITA	From Venice; Latin
VINNIE	Feminine form of Vincent
VIOLA	(Vi) A violet; Latin
VIOLET	(Vi) Violet; French
VIRGINIA	(Ginny, Virgie) Virgin; Latin

VITA, VETA	Animated; Latin
VIVIAN, VIVIENNE	(Viv) Full of life, also used as a masculine name; French
VOLETA, VOLETTA	Veiled one; Old French

W

WAHKUNA	Beautiful; American Indian
WAKENDA	One who worships; American Indian
WALLIS	Feminine for Wallace
WALPURGA	Powerful; Germanic
WALTINA	(Tina) Feminine form of Walter; Teutonic
WANDA	Wanderer; Germanic
WANITA	Variant of Juanita
WANNETTA	Pale one; English
WAPEKA	Skillful; American Indian
WARDENA	A guardian; Germanic
WENDELIN, WENDELINE	(Wendy) Wanderer; Germanic
WENDY	(see Gwendolen)
WILHELMINA	(Mina, Minnie) Feminine form of William; German
WILLETTA	Feminine form of William
WILMA	Feminine form of William; Germanic
WINIFRED	(Winnie) Win peace; Latin

70

WINONA, **WENONA,** **WENONAH**	The first born daughter; American Indian

X

XANTHE	Gold hair; Greek
XANTHIPPE	Yellow horse; Greek
XENIA, ZENA	Visitor; Greek
XIMENA	One who visits; Greek

Y

YASMIN	(see Jasmine)
YETTA	(see Henrietta)
YOLANDA	For the violet; Old French
YVETTE	Archer; French
YVONNE	(Von) Archer; French

Z

ZANDRA	Feminine form of Alexander; One who helps people; Greek
ZELDA	Diminutive of Griselda; Gray; Germanic
ZENA, ZEENA	Variation of Xenia
ZENOTIA	Having life from Jupiter; Greek
ZOE	Life; Greek
ZONA	Belt; Greek
ZORA	Dawn; Slavic
ZULEIKA	The fair one; Arabic

Names for Your Baby Boy

"'Tis pleasant sure to see one's name in print."
Lord Byron

A

AARON	Mountain, light; Hebrew
ABBOT, ABBOTT	(Abbey) Title of respect in Aramaic; Old English, Arabic—Father
ABEL	(Nab) Breath, vanity; Hebrew
ABELARD	Hard, noble; Germanic
ABIJAH	Father is Jehovah; Hebrew
ABNER	(Ab) Of light, wisdom; Hebrew
ABRAHAM	(Abe, Abie) Exalted founder of Hebrew people; Hebrew
ABRAM	(Bram) Original name of Abraham; Hebrew
ABSALOM	Peace; Hebrew
ACE	Together, unity; Latin
ACHILLES	He who is without lips; Greek
ADAIR	From the ford at the oaks; Anglo-Saxon
ADAM	(Ade) Man, red earth (Created from red dust of earth); Hebrew
ADDISON	Son of Adam; Old English
ADELBERT	Bright; Germanic
ADLAI	Living the word of God; Hebrew
ADOLPH	(Adolf, Adolfe) Noble hero; Teutonic
ADRIAN	Dark one (named by fair-haired people); Latin
AHERN, AHERNE	Owns many horses; Gaelic Irish
AINSLEY	The awe-inspiring one's meadow; Old English

ALAN, ALLEN, ALLAN	Cheerful, handsome; Medieval, Middle Latin
ALASTAIR	(Allister) Defender of men; Scotch of Alexander
ALBAN	White; Latin
ALBERT	(Al, Bert) Illustrious, noble; Teutonic
ALBION	Ancient name of England; Celtic
ALDEN, ALDIN	Friend; Anglo-Saxon
ALDIS	(Aldous, Aldus) Ancient home; Old English
ALDO	Old, wise; Germanic
ALDRED	(Al) Old; Anglo-Saxon
ALDRICH	Wise rules; Old English or Germanic
ALDWIN	Old; Anglo-Saxon
ALEXANDER	(Alex, Lex, Aleck) Defender of men; Greek
ALEXIS	(Lex, Alex) Help; Greek
ALFONSO	(Al, Alphonso) River crossing; Germanic, used by early kings of Spain
ALFRED	(Al, Fred, Alf) Good counselor; Anglo-Saxon
ALGER	Spearman; Old German
ALISON	(Al) Noble one's son; Old English
ALOYSIUS	(see Lewis) Famous warrior; Late Latin
ALTON	Old, high town
ALVIN	(Al) Friend, noble; Teutonic
AMBROSE	Immortal; Greek

AMERIGO	(see Emery) Italian explorer
AMORY, AMERY	Ruler; Old German, English (Amery)
AMOS	Born of God; Hebrew
ANATOLE	New to west; Greek
ANDREW	(Andy, Drew) Strong and manly; Greek
ANGELO	(Angie) Messenger; Greek
ANGUS	Unique strength; Scotch Gaelic
ANTHONY, ANTONY	(Tony) Latin
ARCHER	Bowman; Anglo-Saxon
ARCHIBALD	(Archie, Archy, Baldie) Bold; Teutonic
ARMAND	Patron Saint of Netherlands; Old German
ARNEY, ARNIE	(Arnie) Eagle; Old German, English
ARNOLD	(Arnie) Strong as an Eagle; Teutonic
ARTHUR	(Art, Artie) "Noble one"; Welsh
ASHLEY	Meadow; Anglo-Saxon
ATWATER	Dweller at water; Old English
AUBREY	Ruler of the elves; Teutonic
AUGUST	(Gus) Exalted; Latin
AUGUSTINE	Belonging to Augustus; Latin
AUSTIN	(Aus) Kingly; Latin
AVERELL	Month of April; Middle English
AVERY	Elf-ruler; Old English

B

BAILEY	Trusted; Old French
BAIRD	Singer; Irish, Gaelic; English variation, Bard
BALDRIC	Ruler; Germanic
BALDWIN	Bold friend; Teutonic
BARD	Poet; Celtic
BARLOW	Hill; Latin
BARNABUS, BARNABY	(Barnie, Bus) Encouragement; Arabic
BARRETT	Ruler; Germanic
BARRY	Straight; Latin
BARTH	Sheltered; Hebrew
BARTHOL-OMEW	(Bart, Bat) Arabic
BARTRAM	Raven — Viking symbol; Old English
BARUCH	Blessed; Hebrew
BASIL	Kingly, royal; Greek
BAXTER	A baker; Germanic
BAYARD	Knight, powerful; French
BELLAMY	Good friend; Latin
BENEDICT	(Benny, Ben) Blessed; Greek
BENJAMIN	(Ben, Benny, Benjy) Son of the right hand; Greek
BENTLEY	A clearing; Anglo-Saxon
BERMAN	A keeper; Germanic

BERNARD, BARNARD	(Barney, Bernie, Berney) Bold, Teutonic
BERTHOLD	Rules in grandeur; Greek
BERTRAM	Bright raven; Teutonic
BEVAN	Son of Evan; Celtic
BING	From the kettle-shaped hollow; Old German
BLAINE, BLAYNE	Thin, lean; Irish Gaelic
BLAIR	Battle; Gaelic
BLAKE	Fair-haired, fair complexioned; Old English
BLYTHE	Joyous; Anglo-Saxon
BOGART	Bow, strong; Old German
BONAFACE	Lucky; Latin
BOONE	Good one; Old French
BORIS	Warrior; Russian
BOYD	Fair-haired; Celtic
BRADLEY	Broad meadow; Anglo-Saxon
BRANDON	Become tight; Old English
BRANT	Proud one; Old English
BRENDAN	Sword; Gaelic
BRENT	Steep hill; Old English
BRETT	Native of Isle of Brittania; Celtic
BREWSTER	A brewer; German

BRIAN, BRYAN	Irish
BRIGHAM	Dweller at bridge; Middle English
BRODERICK	Son of famous ruler; Middle English
BRONSON	"Son of brown one"; Old English
BRUCE	Dweller at thicket; Old French
BRUNO	Brown; Teutonic
BURL	Cup-bearer; Old English
BURR	Youth; Old Norse
BURTON	Dweller at home; Old English
BYRON	From the cottage or country estate; French

C

CAESAR	Ruler; Latin
CALDWELL	Cold spring; Old English
CALEB	Dog; Hebrew
CALVIN	Bald one; Latin
CAMERON	Crooked nose; Scotch
CARLISLE	City; Old English
CARLO, CARLOS	Italian and Spanish of Charles
CARLTON, CARLETON	(Carl) (see Charles, Karl) Homestead; Old English
CARROL, CARROLL	(see Charles) Latin

CASEY	Brave; Irish Gaelic
CASPAR, CASPER, KASPAR	Treasure master; Greek
CASSIUS	Liberator; Latin (associated with Marcus, Junius, Brutus)
CECIL	Dim-sighted; Latin
CEDRIC	Battle chieftain; Anglo-Saxon
CHAD, CHADWICK, CHAD-BOURNE	Warlike; Old English
CHARLES	(Charlie, Chuck, Chip) Strong, manly; Teutonic
CHARLTON	Farmers' homestead; Old English
CHAUNCEY	A diligent man; French, place name
CHESTER	Camp; English, place name from Latin
CHRISTIAN	(Chris) Follower of Christ; Latin
CHRISTO-PHER	(Chris) Bearing Christ; Greek
CLARE	Bright; Latin
CLARENCE	Bright, famous; Anglo-Saxon
CLARK	Learned; Latin
CLAUDIUS	Lame; Latin
CLAYTON	Clay estate; English, place name
CLEMENT	Mild, merciful; Latin
CLEVELAND	Cliff land; place name

CLIFFORD	Crossing at the cliff; English, place name
CLINTON	(Clint) Hill town; Germanic
CLYDE	Heard from far away; Scottish
CONNELL	Gaelic
CONRAD	Giving bold or wise counsel; Teutonic
CONSTANT	Firm, faithful, true; Latin
CONSTAN-TINE	Faithful; Latin
CORNELIUS	Horn colored; Latin
COURTNEY	Short nose; French
CRAIG, CRAIGE	Dweller at the crag; Scotch Gaelic
CRISPIN	(Cris) Having curly hair; Latin
CULLAM, CULLEN	Handsome one; Gaelic
CUTHBERT	Noted, splendor; Anglo-Saxon
CYRANO	From Cyrene; Greek
CYRIL	Lordly; Greek

D

DALE	Valley; Germanic, "Thal" original form of this name
DALTON	Valley town; English
DAMON	Constant one; Greek
DAN	A judge; Hebrew
DANA	Variation of Dan

DANIEL	"God is my judge"; Hebrew
DANTE	Lasting; Italian, Short form of Durante
DARIUS	Possessing wealth; Persian
DARRYL, DARRELL	Region of wild animals; French
DARREN	Little great one; Gaelic
DAVID	(Dave, Davy) Beloved; Hebrew
DAVIS	Son of beloved one; Old English
DEAN	Valley; Anglo-Saxon, Latin Leader of ten
DEMETRIUS	Of Demeter of earth mother; Greek
DENNIS, DENES	Wine and song (from Dionysus); French
DERRICK	(Dirk) Dutch
DESMOND	Irish, from South Munster (south Irish province)
DEWEY	(see David) Welsh
DEWITT, DeWITT	White; Dutch
DEXTER	Fortunate, On the right hand of God; Latin
DION	Wine and song; Greek
DIRK, DEREK, DIRCK	Anglo-Saxon surname
DOMINIC	Belonging to the Lord; Latin
DONALD	(Don, Donnie) World ruler; Gaelic
DORIAN	An inhabitant of, or pertaining to, the region called Doris or Dorea; English from Greek

DOUGLAS	(Doug) Scottish
DREW	Trusty; Germanic
DUANE	On the downs; Celtic
DUDLEY	From the people's meadow; Old English
DUNCAN	Brown warrior; Gaelic
DWIGHT	A cutting or clearing; Old English
DYLAN	Son of the wave; Welsh

E

EARL	Man, noble; Anglo-Saxon
EBENEZER	(Eben) The stone of help; Hebrew
EDEN	Place of pleasure; Hebrew
EDGAR	Protector of property; Anglo-Saxon
EDISON	Son of Edward; Old English
EDMUND, EDMOND	(Ed, Eddie, Ned) Defender of property; Anglo-Saxon
EDSEL	A prosperous man's manor or hall; Old English
EDWARD	(Ed, Eddie, Ned, Ted, Teddy) Guardian; Anglo-Saxon
EDWIN	Gainer of property; Anglo-Saxon
EGBERT	Bright weapon; Anglo-Saxon
ELDON	From the holy hill; Old English
ELEAZAR, ELEAZER	God has helped; Hebrew
ELI	High; Hebrew

ELIAS	Jehova is God; Greek
ELIHU	God, the Lord; Hebrew
ELIJAH	Jehovah is God; Hebrew
ELIOT, ELLIOTT	Jehovah is my God; Hebrew, French
ELMER	Noble, famous; Anglo-Saxon
ELTON	(see Alton)
EMERY, EMORY	Industrious ruler; Teutonic
EMIL, EMILE	Flattering; French
EMMANUEL	(Manny) God is with us; Hebrew
EMMETT	Industrious, strong; Old German
ENOCH	Dedicated; Hebrew
ENOS	Man; Hebrew
EPHRAIM	Very fruitful; Hebrew
ERASMUS	Beloved; Greek
ERIC	Ever powerful, ever-ruler; Scandinavian
ERNEST, EARNEST	(Ernie) Earnest one; Greek
ERWIN	Sea friend; Old English
ETHAN	Firmness, strength; Hebrew
EUGENE	Well-born of noble race; Greek
EUSTACE	Stable; Greek
EVAN	Young warrior; Welsh
EVELYN	Youth; English

EVERARD	Very strong, wild; Teutonic
EVERETT	Boar-strong; Germanic
EZEKIEL	(Zeke) God makes strong; Hebrew
EZRA	Help; Hebrew

F

FABIAN	Bean grower; Latin
FARLEY	Strong leader; Irish
FARQUHAR	Manly; Gaelic
FAUST	Lucky; Latin
FELIX	Happy, joyous; Latin
FEODOR	A gift; Russian
FERDINAND	Adventurer; Teutonic
FERGUS	Strong; Gaelic
FILMER	Famous; German
FLOYD	Dark-complexioned; Welsh
FRANCHOT	Free; Germanic
FRANCIS	(Frank) Free; Teutonic
FRANKLIN	(Frank, Frankie) Freeman; Middle English
FREDERICK, FREDERIC	(Fred, Freddy, Rick) Teutonic
FRITZ	Peace; Teutonic

G

GABRIEL	(Gabe) Man of God; Hebrew
GAIL, GALE	Lively; Anglo-Saxon
GAMALIEL	Recompense of God; Hebrew
GARCIA	Ruler; Germanic
GARDINER, GARDNER	A gardener; Germanic
GARLAND	Crowned for victory; Old French
GARRET, GARRETT	(Garry, Gary) Gentle; Anglo-Saxon
GARTH, GARETH	A gardener; Anglo-Saxon
GARY, GARRY	Spear, hard; Germanic
GASCON, GASTON	A native of Gascony; Old French
GASPAR	Horseman; Persian
GAVIN	Falcon; Scottish
GAYELORD, GAYLORD	Gay; Old English
GEOFFREY, JEFFREY	(Jeff, Geoff) Peace; Teutonic
GEORGE	(Georgie) Husband, farmer; Greek
GERALD	Warrior; Teutonic
GERARD	Strong with weapons; Teutonic
GERBERT	Bright; Teutonic
GERBOLD	Bold; Teutonic

GERSHOM	Bell; Hebrew
GERVAS, GERVASE	Latin
GIDEON	Feller, Hewer; Hebrew
GIFFORD	Gift; Teutonic
GILBERT	(Gil, Bert, Gib) Bright wish; Teutonic
GILES	Aegis; Old French
GILFORD	Crossing; Irish
GILROY	Servant; Latin
GLENN, GLEN	Glen or valley; Irish
GODDARD	Pious, virtuous; Teutonic
GODFREY	Peace of God; Teutonic
GODWIN	Friend of God; Anglo-Saxon
GORDON	Anglo-Saxon
GRAHAM	Gray house; Anglo-Saxon
GRANT	Large or great; Latin
GRANVILLE	Large village; Old French
GREGORY	(Greg) Vigilant; Greek
GRIFFITH	Fierce lord; Welsh
GROVER	Dweller in the grove; Anglo-Saxon
GUNTHER	Hard; Teutonic
GUSTAVUS	(Gus, Gust) Goth's staff; Swiss
GUY	A leader; French

H

HADRIAN	(see Adrian)
HADWIN	Friend; Germanic
HALBERT	(Hal) Bright; Germanic
HAMILTON	Fortified castle; Place name
HANNIBAL	Grace; Punic
HANS	(see John) Hebrew
HARLAN, HARLAND	Land; Germanic
HARLEY	Long field; Place name
HAROLD	(Hal) Army-leader; Anglo-Saxon
HARRISON	Son of Harry; Germanic
HARRY	(see Harold and Henry) Battle; Germanic
HARTLEY	Meadow; Germanic
HARVEY	Army battle; Germanic
HECTOR	(Heck) Holding tight; Greek
HEMAN	Faithful; Hebrew
HENRY	(Harry, Hal) Ruler of private property; Teutonic
HERBERT	(Bert, Herb) Glory of the Army; Anglo-Saxon
HERMAN	A warrior; Teutonic
HEZEKIAL	God has strengthened; Hebrew
HILARY	Cheerful, merry; Latin
HIRAM	Most noble; Phoenician

HIROSHI	Generous; Japanese
HO	Good; Chinese
HOBART	(Bart) Bright; Germanic
HOMER	Pledge; Greek
HORACE	On time; Latin
HORATIO	On time; Latin
HOSEA	Salvation; Hebrew
HOWARD	(Howie) Strong; Germanic
HOWELL	Important; Welsh
HUBERT	Bright in spirit; Teutonic
HUGH	(Huey, Hughie) Mind; Teutonic
HUMBERT	Giant, bright; Germanic
HUMPHREY	Giant, peace; Anglo-Saxon
HURD	Strong; Old English
HYMAN	(Hymie) Life; Hebrew

I

IAGO	May God protect; Hebrew (Spanish form of James)
IAN	Gaelic form of John
IBRAHIM	Faithful; Arabic
ICHABOD	Inglorious; Hebrew
IGNATIUS	Greek
IGOR	Hero; Germanic

ILBERT	Brightness; Germanic
INGRAM	Angel; Germanic
IMMANUEL	(see Emanuel)
IRA	Watchful; Hebrew
IRVING, IRVIN	(Irv) Beautiful; Old English
IRWIN	Sea friend; Anglo-Saxon
ISAAC	(Ike, Ikey) Laughter; Hebrew
ISAIAH	Salvation of the Lord; Hebrew
ISIDORE	Gift of Isis; Greek
ISRAEL	Contender with God; Hebrew
IVAN	Russian for John
IVAR, IVOR	Hero; Germanic
IVON	Bowman; Hebrew

J

JABEZ	He will cause pain; Hebrew
JACK	Form of John and Jacob
JACQUES	French form of James
JACOB	A supplanter; Hebrew
JAMES	A supplanter; Hebrew from Jacob
JAN	Dutch form for John
JAPHETH	Enlargement; Hebrew
JARIUS	He will enlighten; Hebrew

JARRED	Descent; Hebrew
JARVIS, JERVIS	From a surname
JASON	Healer; Greek
JASPER	Treasurer; French
JAY	Form of Jacob and Jason
JEFFREY	(Jeff) (see Geoffrey)
JEREMIAH, JEREMY	(Jerry) Exalted of the Lord; Hebrew
JEROME	(Jerry) Bearing a holy name; Greek
JERROLD	(see Gerald)
JERRY	Form of Gerald and Jerome
JESSE	(Jess) Gift of God; Hebrew
JETHRO	Eminence; Hebrew
JOAB	Jehovah is his father; Hebrew
JOB	Afflicted, persecuted; Hebrew
JOCELIN, JOCELYN	Merry; Latin
JOCK	Scottish form of Jack
JOEL	The Lord is God; Hebrew
JOHN	(Johnny, Jack) God is gracious; Hebrew
JONAH	A dove; Hebrew
JONAS	A dove; Hebrew
JONATHAN	(Jon, Johnny, Jack, Nat) God has given; Hebrew

JORDAN	Land; Hebrew
JOSEPH	(Joe, Joey) He shall add; Hebrew
JOSHUA	(Josh) Jehovah supports; Hebrew
JOTHAN	Jehovah is perfect; Hebrew
JOYCE	Merry; Latin
JUDAH	Praised; Hebrew
JUDE	Praise; Hebrew
JULIAN	Sprung from Julius; Latin
JULIUS	Youthful; Latin
JUSTIN	Just; Latin

K

KARL	(see Charles) German
KASPER	Horseman; Persian
KEANE, KEENE	Ancient; Irish
KEITH	Enclosed place; Scottish
KELVIN	A warrior friend; Celtic
KEMPER	(Kemp) Warrior; Germanic
KENNETH	(Ken, Kenny) Handsome; Anglo-Saxon
KENT	Open country; English
KENWARD	Brave; Old English
KERMIT	Free; Celtic
KERRY	Dark; Celtic

KERWIN	Friend; Germanic
KESTER	(see Christopher) Greek
KEVEN, KEVIN	Handsome; Irish
KIM	Chief; Celtic
KING	Ruler; Anglo-Saxon
KIRBY	Churchtown; English
KIRK	Church; Celtic
KIT	(see Christopher)
KNUD	Kind; Danish
KONARD	(see Conrad)
KURT	Form of Conrad
KYLE	Handsome; Gaelic

L

LABAN	White; Hebrew
LAFAYETTE	From a surname
LAIRD	Land owner; Celtic
LAMBERT	(Bert) Illustrious with landed possessions; Teutonic
LANCE, LANCELOT	Land; French
LARS	Lord; Etruscan
LAURENCE, LAWRENCE	(Larry) The Laurel; Latin
LAZARUS	Grace; Hebrew

LEANDER	A lion; Greek
LEAR	The sea; Celtic
LEE, LEIGH	Meadow; From a surname
LELAND	(Lee) Meadow; Anglo-Saxon
LEMUEL	Consecrated to God; Hebrew
LEO	Lion; Latin
LEOFRIC	Ruler; Old English
LEOFWIN	Friend; Old English
LEON	Lion; Latin
LEONARD	Strong as a lion; Greek
LEONIDAS	Lionlike; Greek
LEOPOLD	Bold for the people; Teutonic
LEROY	Royal; French
LESLIE	Law meadow; From a surname
LESTER	(Les) Camp; From a surname
LEVI	Joining; Hebrew
LEWIS	Warrior; Germanic
LINCOLN	Lake; Latin, from a surname
LINDSAY, LINDSEY	Hedge; Old English
LINUS	Flaxen-haired; Greek
LIONEL	(Lin) Young lion; French
LLEWELYN	Like a lion; Welsh
LLOYD	Gray; Welsh

LOGAN	Hollow meadow; Celtic
LORRANZO	Italian for Lawrence
LOT	An envelope; Hebrew
LOUIS	Famous warrior; Teutonic
LOWELL	Little wolf; Latin
LUCIUS	Light; Latin
LUDLOW	One from Ludlow; Old English
LUDWIG	Glory; Germanic
LUKE, LUCAS	Light; Greek
LUTHER	Illustrious warrior; Greek
LYLE	From the island; French
LYMAN	From the valley; Place name, Old English
LYNN	Mountain torrent; Anglo-Saxon

M

MAC	Diminutive of any name beginning with Mc or Mac; Celtic
MAGNUS	Great; Latin
MAHLON	Sickness; Hebrew
MALACHI	Messenger; Hebrew
MALCOLM	Servant of Columbia; Gaelic
MALLORY	The mailed; Latin
MALVIN, MELVIN	Servant; Celtic
MANCHU	Pure; Chinese

MANDEL	Pleasure; Germanic
MANFRED	Peace; Germanic
MANLEY, MANLY	Virile; Germanic
MANUEL	(Manny) God with us; Spanish
MANVILLE, MANVEL	From the large estate; Latin
MARCELLUS	Diminutive of Marcus; From the god, Mars; Latin
MARCH	Horse; Anglo-Saxon
MARCO	From the god, Mars, Italian for Mark; Latin
MARCUS, MARC, MARK	From the god, Mars; Latin
MARIO	From the god, Mars, wished-for child, masculine form of Mary; Latin
MARION	Bitterness, masculine form of Mary; French
MARIUS	For the god, Mars; Latin
MARLIN, MERLIN	Sea-hill; Old English
MARLOWE	Hill by the lake; Teutonic
MARMADUKE	(Duke) Sea leader; Celtic
MARSHALL	An official in charge of horses; Old French
MARSTON	Homestead by a marsh; Old English
MARTIAL	Warlike; Latin

MARTIN	(Marty, Mart) Warlike; Latin
MARVIN	(Marv) Friend; Germanic
MATTHEW	(Matt) Gift of Jehovah; Hebrew
MAURICE	(Maury) Dark; Latin
MAXMILLIAN	(Max) The greatest; Latin
MAXWELL	(Max) Big spring; Anglo-Saxon
MAYNARD	Hard, strength; Germanic
MELDON	Valley; Old English
MELVILLE	Hill; Anglo-Saxon
MERLE	Blackbird; French
MERLIN	Sea; Celtic
MERRILL	(see Muriel) Celtic
MERTON	Lovely sea; Anglo-Saxon
MERVYN	Related to Merlin
MERWIN	Friend of the sea; Germanic
MEYER	Farmer; Germanic
MICAH	Who is like God; Hebrew
MICHAEL	(Mike) Who is like God; Hebrew
MIGUEL	(see Michael) Spanish
MILES	Merciful; Teutonic
MILTON	(Milt, Miltie) From a surname
MITCHELL	From a surname; Hebrew
MONROE	Mouth of the Roe River; Celtic
MONTAGUE	Sharp mountain; Latin

MORGAN	Dweller in the sea; Welsh
MORRIS	Feminine form of Maura; Latin
MORTIMER	(Mort, Morty) Still water; French
MORTON	(Mort) Village on the moor; Anglo-Saxon
MOSES	Child; Egyptian
MURRAY	Merry; From a surname; English
MYRON	Fragrant; Greek

N

NAAMAN	Pleasantness; Hebrew
NAHUM	Comforter; Hebrew
NAPOLEON	A lion; Italian, Greek
NATHAN	(Nat, Nate) Gift, given; Hebrew
NATHANIEL	(Nat) Gift of God; Hebrew
NEAL, NEIL	Courageous; Gaelic
NEHEMIAH	Comfort of Jehovah; Hebrew
NELSON	(Sonny) From a surname; Anglo-Saxon
NESTOR	One who remembers; Greek
NEVILLE, NEVIL, NEVILE	(Nev) New city; Latin
NEVIN, NEVINS	A nephew; Old English
NEWBOLD	Place name; English
NEWELL	Latin

NIAL, NIEL	A champion; Celtic
NICHOLAS	(Nick, Nicky) Victorious army; Greek
NICODEMUS	(Nick) The victor; Egyptian
NIGEL	Black; Gaelic
NILES	The son of Neil; Danish
NINIAN	The sky; Latin
NOAH	Rest, comfort; Hebrew
NOBLE	Well-born; Latin
NOEL, NOLL	Christmas; Latin
NOLAND	Noble; Latin
NOLL	(see Noel)
NORBERT	(Bert) God of the sea; Germanic
NORMAN	(Norm) A Northman; Scandinavian
NORRIS	Surname, from the north; Anglo-Saxon
NORTON	From the north; Place name
NORVAL	Valley in the north; Germanic
NOWELL	Christmas; Latin

O

OBADIAH	Servant of the Lord; Hebrew
OCTAVIUS, OCTAVIAN	The eighth born; Latin
ODO	Wealthy; Germanic
OGDEN	Oak valley; Old English

OLAF	(Olie, Ollid) Ancestor; Norse
OLIN	(see Olaf)
OLIVER	(Ollie) Olive tree; Latin
OMAR	A builder; Hebrew
OMER	Wealthy; Germanic
ORA	Gold-like; Latin
ORIN, OREN	White skin; Hebrew
ORLANDO	Fame of the land; Italian
ORSON	The bear; Latin
ORTON	Hill town; Old English
ORVILLE	Town of gold; French
OSBERT	Bright, Os (a god); Anglo-Saxon
OSBORN	Os (a god), divine bear; Anglo-Saxon
OSCAR	Os (a god), godlike spear; Anglo-Saxon
OSGOOD	Extremely good, as from God or the heavens; Anglo-Saxon
OSMOND, OSMUND	Power of God; Anglo-Saxon
OSRIC	Os (a god), divine ruler; Germanic
OSWALD	Divine ruler; Anglo-Saxon
OTIS	(see Otto)
OTTO	(Ott) Wealthy; Greek
OWEN	A young warrior; Welsh

P

PABLO	Spanish for Paul
PADDY	Diminutive of Patrick
PADRAIC	Irish for Patrick
PAGE	Boy servant; Greek
PALEY	Little; Latin
PALMER	A pilgrim; Latin
PARK, PARKE	Keeper of the pork; French
PARRY	Son of Harry; Welsh
PASCAL	Born of suffering; Hebrew
PATRICK	(Pat, Paddy) Noble, a patrician; Latin
PAUL	Little; Latin
PAYNE	Surname; Latin
PAYTON	Noble; Latin
PEDRO	Spanish for Peter
PERCIVAL, PERCEVAL	(Percy) Perceive the veil; French
PERCY	From a surname; Anglo-Saxon
PEREGRINE	(Perry) A wanderer; Latin
PERRY	From a surname; Anglo-Saxon
PETER	(Pete) Solid, like stone; Greek
PHELIM	Always good; Celtic
PHELPS	(see Phillip) Anglo-Saxon surname
PHEODOR	From God; Greek
PHILANDER	(Phil) A lover of men; Greek

PHILBERT	(Phil, Bert) Bright; Germanic
PHILEMON	(Phil) Loving; Greek
PHILETUS	(Phil) Affectionate; Greek
PHILIP, PHILLIP	(Phil, Flip) Horse man and lover of horses; Greek
PHINEAS	Mouth of brass; Hebrew
PIERRE	French for Peter
PIUS	Pious; Latin
POMPEY	From Pompeii; Latin
POSTUMUS	The last; Latin
POWELL	From Howell; Celtic
PRESCOTT	Priest's cottage; Old English
PRESTON	Priest-place; Old English
PRICE	The son of Rice; Welsh

Q

QUARTUS	The fourth; Latin
QUERTON	Dark; Celtic
QUILLON	Cross quard of a sword; Latin
QUINCY	The fifth; Latin
QUINN	Wise one; Celtic
QUINTILIAN	Roman surname
QUINTIN, QUENTIN	The fifth; Latin
QUINTUS	The fifth; Latin

101

R

RADCLIFFE	A red cliff; Old English
RADFORD	Red river crossing; Old English
RALPH, RAOUL, ROLF	(Rafe) Wolf-counsel; Latin
RAMON	Spanish for Raymond
RAMSEY, RAMSAY	Wooded island; Old English
RANDALL, RANDAL	(Rand, Randy, Ran) Shield-wolf; Old English
RANDOLPH	(Randy) See Randall
RANGER	A guard of the forest; Anglo-Saxon
RANULF	Wolf; Germanic
RAOUL	Wolf-counsel; Germanic
RAPHAEL	God has healed; Hebrew
RASTUS	Will not leave; Greek
RAYMOND	(Ray) Wise protection; Teutonic
RAYNARD	(Ray) War-counsel; Germanic
RAYNER	(Ray) War-counsel; Germanic
REDMOND, REDMUND	(Ed) Protector; Germanic
REED, REID	Red; Old English
REGAN	King; Celtic
REGINALD	(Reggie) Strong ruler; Teutonic
REINHOLD	Power; Germanic
RENE	Reborn; French

RENFRED	(Fred) Peace; Germanic
REUBAN	Behold a son; Hebrew
REUEL	God is his friend; Hebrew
REX	King; Latin
REXFORD	(Rex) Crossing of the king; Latin
REYNOLD	Mighty; Germanic
RICHARD	(Rich, Ricky, Dick, Dicky, Richie) A strong ruler, powerful; Teutonic
RIP	Nickname for Robert
ROALD	Famous; Germanic
ROBERT	(Rob, Robbie, Bob, Bobby, Robin) Bright in fame; Teutonic
ROBIN	(Rob) Diminutive for Robert
ROBINSON	(Rob, Robbie) Son of Robert; Anglo-Saxon
ROCKY	For Italian Rocco
RODERICK	(Rod, Roddy) Rich in fame; Teutonic
RODMAN	(Rod, Roddy) A helper; Germanic
RODNEY	(Rod, Roddy) Servant; Anglo-Saxon
ROGER	(Roge) Famous with the spear; Teutonic
ROLAND	Fame of the land; Teutonic
ROLF	Fame-wolf; Germanic
ROLLO	Short for Rudolph; Germanic
ROMAIN, ROMANE	From Rome; Latin
ROMEO	Strong; Latin

RONALD, RONOLD	(Ron, Ronnie) Mighty; Scottish
ROOSEVELT	(Rosie) Field of roses; Dutch
RORY	Red; Irish
ROSCOE	From a surname
ROSS	Red; Gaelic
ROSWELL, ROSWOLD	Strength; Germanic
ROY	King; French
ROYAL	(Roy) King; French
RUBY, RUBIN	Red; Latin
RUDOLPH	(Rudy) Wolf; famous; Teutonic
RUDYARD	Wolf, famous; Germanic
RUFUS	Red-haired; Latin
RUPERT	(see Robert) Germanic
RUSSELL	(Russ, Rusty) From a surname; Anglo-Saxon
RUTHERFORD	Red-crossing; Scottish
RYAN	From a surname; Anglo-Saxon
RYDER	From a surname; Anglo-Saxon

S

SABIN	From an Italian tribe; Latin
SALMON	Peace; Hebrew
SAM	(see Samuel)

SAMSON, SAMPSON	(Sam) Solai; sun's man; Hebrew
SAMUEL	(Sam, Sammy) His name is God; Hebrew
SANDERS	(see Alexander)
SANDOR	A helper of man; Greek
SANFORD	A sandy river crossing; Old English
SAUL	Asked for; Hebrew
SAWYER	One who cuts timber; Anglo-Saxon
SAXON	A swordsman; Germanic
SCHUYLER	Scholar, from a surname; Dutch
SCOTT	A native of Scotland; English
SEABROOK	Brook running from the sea; Anglo-Saxon
SEAN SHAWN	Irish form of John
SEARLE	Armed; Germanic
SEBA	(see Sebastian) Greek
SEBASTIAN	Venerable; Greek
SEBERT	Victorious; Germanic
SEBOND	Victorious; Germanic
SEDWICK	Victory-town; Germanic
SELBY	From Yorkshire; Anglo-Saxon
SELDEN	Anglo-Saxon
SELIG	Blessed; Germanic
SELWYN	Palace; Anglo-Saxon
SEMAR	Victorious; Germanic

SENIOR, SYNYER	The Father; Latin
SEPTINUS	The seventh; Latin
SERGE, SERGIUS	To serve; Latin
SETH	Appointed; Hebrew
SEUMAS	Irish for James
SEWARD	Victorious, from a surname; Anglo-Saxon
SEWELL	Victorious; Teutonic
SEXTUS	The sixth; Latin
SEYMOUS	Sea, from a surname; French
SHANUS	Irish for James; Hebrew
SHAWN, SHANE	For John; Irish
SHELBY	Homestead; Old English
SHELDON	A hut on the hill; Old English
SHEPARD, SHEPPARD	A shepherd; Old English
SHERARD	Bright; Old English
SHERLOCK	Fair-haired; Old English
SHERMAN	A cutter of cloth; Old English
SHERWIN	Bright; Old English
SIBLEY	A prophet; Latin
SIDNEY, SYDNEY	(Sid) From St. Denis, also girl's name; English

SIEGFRIED	(Sig, Siggy) Victory, peace; German
SIGISMUND	Conquering protection; Teutonic
SIGRID	Victory, peace; Old Norse
SIGURD	Victory, peace; Old Norse
SIGWALD	Victory, rule; Old Norse
SILAS	Woodland; Latin
SILVANUS	Living in a wood; Latin
SILVESTER	Bred in the country; Latin
SIMEON	Hearing; Hebrew
SIMON	(Sy, Sim) Snub-nosed; Hebrew
SINCLAIR	(Sinc) Saint; Latin
SIVARD	Victory, protector; Old English
SOL	The sun; Latin
SOLOMAN	Peaceful; Hebrew
SOLON	A wise man; Greek
SPENCER	(Spence) House steward; Old English
STACEY, STACY	One who shall rise again; Greek
STAFFORD	A stony river crossing; Old English
STANFORD	A stony river crossing; Old English
STANISLOUS	Camp glory; Polish
STANLEY	(Stan) Stone field, from a surname; Old English
STANTON	Stony town; Old English

STEPHEN, STEVEN, STEFAN	(Steve, Stevie) Crown, feminine form is Stephanie; Greek
STERLING	Excellent; English
STEWART, STUART	Caretaker, from a surname; Old English
STUYVESANT	Dutch
SUMNER	Of the forest; Latin
SYLVANUS	Of the forest; Latin
SYLVESTER	Of the forest; Latin

T

TABER	(Tab, Tabb) Drummer; French
TAD	(see Thaddeus)
TALBOT	A bright valley; English
TAYLOR	Cutter; French
TEAGUE	A poet; Celtic
TED	(see Theodore and Edward)
TEDMAN	Protection; Germanic
TERENCE	(Terry) Tender; Latin
TERTIUS	The third; Latin
THADDEUS	(Thad, Tad) Praiseworthy; Greek
THANE	Warrior, landed gentry; Old English
THAYER	Pastureland; English

THEOBOLD	(Ted) Bold; Teutonic
THEODORE	(Ted, Teddy) Ruler; Teutonic
THEOPHILUS	Dear to the Gods; Greek
THERON	A hunter; Greek
THOMAS	(Tom, Tommy) A twin; Hebrew
THOR	Thunder; Norwegian
THORNTON	Thorntown; Norwegian
THURMAN	Thor's protection; Norwegian
THURSTON	Thor's stone; Scandinavian
TIFFANY	God appears; Greek
TIMOTHY	(Tim, Timmy) Honoring God; Greek
TITUS	Safe; Greek
TOBIAH, TOBIAS	The Lord is my good; Hebrew
TOD, TODD	Fox; Scottish
TONY	Diminutive of Anthony; Latin
TORIN	Chief; Irish
TRACEY, TRACY	Village; French
TRAVERE, TRAVIS	Crossroad; Latin
TRELAWNY	Church town; Germanic
TREVOR	Prudent; Welsh
TRISTRAM	Bold; Celtic
TROY	From the city; Greek

TRUEMAN, TRUMAN	Faithful; Anglo-Saxon
TULLY	Orator; Latin
TYBALT	(see Theobald)
TYRONE	Land of Owen; Irish

U

ULICK	Rewarder; Scandinavian
ULRIC	Wolf; Germanic
ULYSSES	A hater; Greek
UPTON	From the hill town; English
URBAN	"Of the city"; Latin
URIAH	My light is Jehovah; Hebrew
URIEL	Light of God; Hebrew

V

VACHEL	Keeper of the cows; French
VALENTINE	Strong, healthy, powerful; Latin
VALERIAN, VALERIA	(Val) Courageous, healthy; Latin
VAN, VANCE	Son of Van; Dutch
VANYA	Form of John; Russian
VARDER, VARDON	A green hill; French
VAUGH	Small; Welsh

VERGIL, VIRGIL	Flourishing; Latin
VERNON	(Vern) Like spring; French
VICTOR	(Vic) Conqueror; Latin
VINCENT	(Vince, Vinny) Conquering; Latin
VIVIAN, VIVIEN, VIVIENNE	(Viv, Vivi) From a surname, also girl's name; French
VLADIMIR	Prince of the world; Slavic

W

WADE	A mover; English
WADSWORTH	Home of Wado; Old English
WALDEMAR	Famous; Germanic
WALDEN	Strong; Germanic
WALDFORD	Advance; Old English
WALDO	Mighty; Germanic
WALLACE	(Wally) Stranger; Anglo-Saxon
WALMAR	Ruler; Germanic
WALMUND	Ruler; protector; Germanic
WALTER	(Walt, Wally) Ruling the host; Teutonic
WARD	Guard; Germanic
WARE	Perceptive; Old English
WARING	Protecting; Germanic
WARNER, WERNER	A friend; Germanic

WARREN	One who protects; Germanic
WARRICK, WARWICK	A farm by a dam; Old English
WASHINGTON	Surname; Old English
WAYLAND	Land by the road; Old English
WAYNE	Diminutive of Wainwright; Anglo-Saxon
WENDELL, WENDEL	A wanderer; Germanic
WESLEY	(Wes) West field; Anglo-Saxon
WHITELAW	White hill; Old English
WHITNEY	White island; English
WILBUR	(Wil) See Gilbert; Teutonic
WILEY, WYLIE	Water meadow; English
WILFORD	Will peace; Anglo-Saxon
WILFRED	Desire for peace; Teutonic
WILHELM	For William; German
WILL	Diminutive for William
WILLARD	(Will, Willy) Strong-willed; Germanic
WILLIAM	(Will, Willy, Bill, Billy) Resolute helmet; Teutonic
WILLIS	Son of William; Germanic
WILLOUGHBY	A home in the willows; Old English
WILMER	Famous; Germanic
WILMOT	Moody; Germanic
WILSON	Son of Will

WILTON	(Wilt) From a surname; Anglo-Saxon
WINFRED, WINFRID	(Win) Peace; Germanic
WINGARD	(Win) Who guards a friend; Germanic
WINSLOW	(Win, Winny) Old English
WINSTON, WINTON	(Win, Winny) Village wine; Old English
WINTHROP	Wine village; Old English
WIRT	A host; English
WOLFRAM	Wolf; Germanic
WOODROW	Path in the woods; English
WRIGHT	A worker; English
WYNDHAM	Path to the home; Anglo-Saxon
WYSTAN	Battle, stone; Anglo-Saxon

X

XANTHUS	Golden-haired; Latin
XAVIER	(Savy) Splendid; Arabic
XENOPHON	Strange voice; Greek
XERXES	Emperor; Greek—Persian
XIMENES	From Simeon; Spanish

Y

YALE	Surname; Welsh
YANCEY	Yankee; French